SOLVE IT WITH SCIENCE

KIDNAPS

ANNE ROONEY

A⁺

Smart Apple Media

Smart Apple Media
P.O. Box 3263, Mankato, Minnesota 56002

Printed in China

Published by arrangement with Arcturus Publishing.

Library of Congress Cataloging-in-Publication Data

Rooney, Anne.
  Kidnaps / Anne Rooney.
    p. cm. – (Solve it with science)
  Includes index.
  ISBN 978-1-59920-331-7 (hardcover)
  1. Kidnapping–Juvenile literature. 2. Kidnapping–
Case studies–Juvenile literature. I. Title.
  HV6595.R66 2010
  364.15'40922–dc22
                                    2009002336

Series concept: Alex Woolf
Editor and picture researcher: Alex Woolf
Designer: Tall Tree

The illustrations on pages 34 and 35 are by Jason Line.

Picture credits:

Arcturus: 34, 35.
Corbis: 4 (Bettmann/John Blair), 6 (Handout/Reuters),
10 (Bettmann), 13 (Bettmann), 15 (Bettmann), 27
(Bettmann), 29 (Bettmann), 42 (Noel Laura/Corbis
Sygma).
FLPA: 20 (Martin B Withers).
Getty: 12 (BIPS Stringer), 14 (Keystone/Stringer), 16
(Time & Life Pictures/Francis Miller/Stringer), 26
(Consolidated News Pictures), cover right and 28
(Keystone/Stringer), 30 (Central Press/Stringer), 41
(Michael Smith/Staff), 43 (Paula Bronstein/Staff).
Rex Features: 38, 39, 40 (KPA/Zuma).
Science Photo Library: 5 (Dr Jurgen Scriba), 7
(Philippe Psaila), 9 (Tek Image), 11 (Paul Rapson), 17
(Philippe Psaila), 19 (Steve Allen), 25 (Volker
Steger/Peter Arnold Inc), 31 (Mauro Fermariello), 33
(Philippe Psaila), 36 (Charles D Winters).
Selbst Fotografiert: 8 (Michael Zaschka).
Shutterstock: cover left (prism_68), 22 (Lagui), 23 top
(Brasiliao-media), 23 bottom (trufero).
TopFoto: 18, 21, 32.

J 364.15
Roo
l/lo

9 8 7 6 5 4 3 2 1

CONTENTS

INTRODUCTION

Kidnapping is a terrifying crime. **Victims** are snatched from their normal life and often held for days, not knowing if they will get out alive. The kidnappers may demand a **ransom**—often money—in exchange for their prisoner.

If a kidnapping goes smoothly, the ransom is paid and the victim is freed. But all too often, it goes wrong. Many investigations end up looking for a murderer.

FIRST STEPS

There are often several **crime scenes** in a kidnapping. There may be little **evidence** left where the person was snatched. More often, the place the person was held—or the place the body was found—holds more clues.

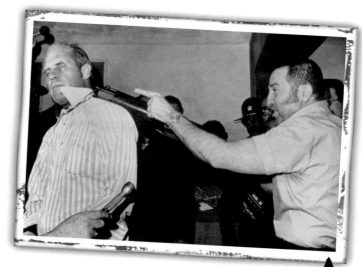

A kidnapper demands money while pointing a shotgun at a hostage.

As with all crimes, it is important that the first people at the scene do not disturb any evidence. Police should seal the area immediately and wait for the **crime scene investigators** (CSIs) to arrive. CSIs take photographs or videos, make measurements, draw sketches, gather physical evidence, and collect any **fingerprints**, footprints, or other marks.

A forensic scientist takes a sample from blood-stained clothing found at a crime scene.

This does not always happen. Family members may discover a relative has been kidnapped. They may find a ransom note and search for any trace of the victim. Valuable evidence is often destroyed before the police even arrive.

FORENSICS WORK

Away from the crime scene, the forensics team works on the evidence the CSIs have collected.

The principle behind forensics is that every contact leaves a trace. The criminal leaves evidence at the crime scene and takes away evidence on his or her body and clothes. The victim also leaves and takes away evidence. The job of forensic scientists is to find the evidence and unravel the crime.

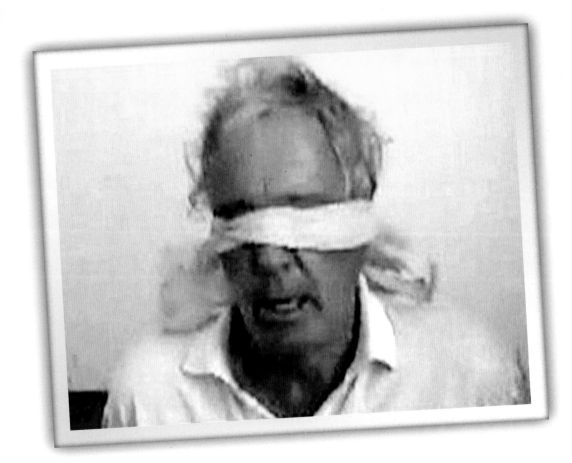

Terrorists who kidnapped and held Kenneth Bigley hostage in Iraq in 2004 posted a video of him on the Internet.

KIDNAPS THROUGH HISTORY

Kidnapping is not a new crime. It has occured for many hundreds of years. In the Middle Ages, armies captured enemy soldiers to hold as **hostages**. They demanded a ransom or the release of other prisoners in exchange for those they had caught.

Wartime kidnapping still occurs today, particularly in the Middle East where there are many **disputes**. **Terrorist** gangs often take hostages and demand political change or the release of prisoners.

In many kidnappings, victims are snatched from their homes or the street and a ransom is demanded for their release. This happens all over the world. In parts of South America, it is so common that kidnapping gangs work like businesses. They snatch wealthy businessmen and **negotiate** ransom. There are even professional negotiators that victims' families can pay to deal with the kidnappers.

FORENSICS

Forensic scientists use many tools to investigate a kidnapping. They examine evidence that might link a person to the crime. Examples include tiny amounts of soil, pollen from plants, fibers, or flakes of paint. Forensic scientists may identify kidnappers from traces of hair, blood, skin, or **DNA**. The evidence at a crime scene may be linked to other objects or people. A bullet at a crime scene may be linked to a particular gun. A handwritten ransom note may match a suspect's writing. Forensics is a fascinating and essential job.

COMPUTER FORENSICS

One of the newest forms of forensic investigation looks for evidence in computer files. Experts can recreate files that have been deleted, even from disks that have been partly destroyed. They can trace Web sites a suspect has visited. This can be vital evidence by showing that someone researched a particular technique or location.

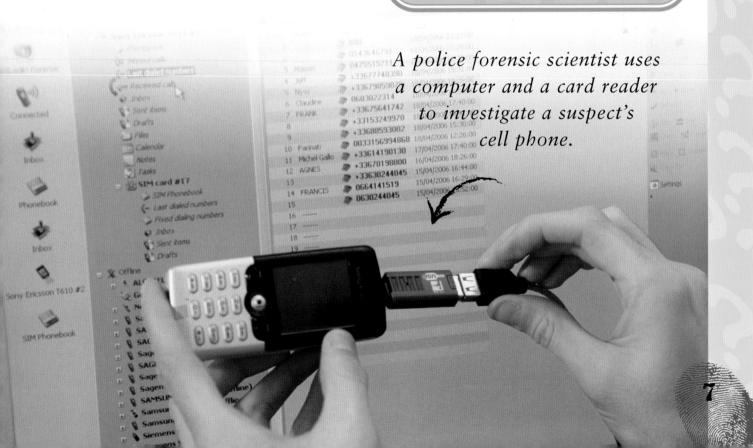

A police forensic scientist uses a computer and a card reader to investigate a suspect's cell phone.

7

KASPAR HAUSER

Kaspar Hauser appeared in a street in Nuremberg, Germany, in 1828. He was a teenager who hardly spoke and knew very little about the world. When he was given paper, he wrote down the name Kaspar Hauser.

A statue of Kaspar Hauser in the city of Ansbach, Germany

THE BOY FROM NOWHERE

After learning to speak, Kaspar said he did not know where he came from. He said that he had been kept in a small cage all his life, and he never saw other people. He had eaten only bread and water.

Kaspar brought two notes with him. One claimed to be from his mother, the other from the man who had kept him prisoner. Investigators examined the handwriting. They determined both notes were written by the same person.

Investigators usually try to find the kidnapper. This time, they tried to find out who Kaspar was.

WAS HE ROYAL?

During Kaspar's life, some people said he was the son of a German duke. They thought he had been taken from his mother as a baby and kept in a **dungeon** by a relative who wanted her own son to become duke.

In 2002, scientists examined **samples** of blood and hair taken from Kaspar's clothes. They extracted DNA from these and compared it with DNA samples from the royal family of Baden. They found a very good match. It seems the stories were true after all.

DNA ANALYSIS

DNA is the chemical material that holds the genetic code for a particular person. Like a fingerprint, everyone's DNA is slightly different. DNA has long strands with a pattern of repeating parts. Scientists compare the patterns in two DNA samples. If they find matches in certain areas, they can be fairly certain the people who provided the samples are related.

The pattern of dark and light bands on this printout is unique—it matches only one person's DNA.

MARIAN PARKER

On December 15, 1927, a man entered Mount Vernon Junior High School in Los Angeles, California. He told teachers he worked for the father of one of their pupils, 12-year-old Marian Parker. The man said Marian's father was ill and wished to see her. Marian left with him. No one realized she was missing until the evening.

The kidnapper sent a ransom demand. Marian's father delivered the money and thought he could see his daughter sitting tied up in a car. The kidnapper dumped Marian and drove off. But to her father's horror, she was already dead.

William Hickman kidnapped and murdered Marian Parker.

A CLEAN SHIRT

Marian was wrapped in a shirt. A laundry mark on it led police to a Los Angeles apartment. They questioned the man living there and searched the apartment, but they found no evidence.

FINGERPRINTS

A fingerprint is the pattern of ridges on the fingertip. Everyone has different fingerprints, even identical twins. When someone touches something, oil from the skin on their fingers leaves a finger print—an invisible record of the ridges of the fingertip.

LIFTING FINGERPRINTS

In 1928, detectives would have dusted powder on the car and the ransom note to find fingerprints (called **latent fingerprints**). The detective carefully laid a special sticky tape over the print to **lift** the powder with the pattern without disturbing it.

Fingerprints lifted at a crime scene are compared with prints taken from a suspect. In 1928, this was done by inking each finger and then rolling the fingertip slowly over paper. Fingerprints are labeled and kept in a file to compare with fingerprints found at a crime scene.

PRINTS ON THE CAR

Police found the car the kidnapper had used. They took fingerprints from the car and found they matched prints on record for a thief, William Hickman. Police found and arrested Hickman. His fingerprints were also on the ransom note. He was convicted of kidnap and murder and **hanged** in 1928.

A forensics officer dusts a car window for fingerprints at a crime scene. The officer is using a powerful lamp to reveal the fingerprints.

CHARLES LINDBERGH JR.

Charles Lindbergh was a famous American aviator who lived in Hopewell, New Jersey. On the evening of March 1, 1932, Lindbergh's 20-month-old son was stolen from his bed. The kidnapper left a ransom note on the windowsill. Outside the window, a broken wooden ladder lay on the ground.

The ransom was paid and Lindbergh was told the baby was being kept on a boat called *Nelly*. There was no such boat. The baby's body was found on land near the house, half buried.

Charles Augustus Lindbergh Junior

EVIDENCE

There were several pieces of evidence at the scene. The kidnapper had left the ladder, made muddy footprints, and dropped an old chisel.

The ladder was an important clue. It was homemade, quite badly, and it just reached the window. Investigators decided it had been made especially for the job. The top rung was broken.

CLUES IN THE WOOD

A wood expert, Arthur Koehler, identified the types of wood used to make the ladder. Examining the wood under a microscope, he found a distinctive pattern of planing. That helped police trace it to a **saw mill** in South Carolina. They learned that some of the wood had been sold to a dealer in the Bronx, New York. But there was no record of who had bought the wood.

EXPERT WITNESS

Forensics work often draws on the knowledge of an expert in a particular field. Arthur Koehler was an expert on wood and trees. He was an **expert witness** in the trial. Examining the wood with a microscope, he found a pattern of grooves from which he worked out the type of **milling machine** used at the saw mill. That helped police trace the wood. His work also revealed marks that matched the wood to a plane in the garage of suspect Bruno Hauptmann. This, and the nail holes that matched wood from Hauptmann's attic, were enough to link the ladder with Hauptmann.

Arthur Koehler is pictured with the kidnapper's ladder and a board taken from Hauptmann's attic. Koehler is pointing to a nail hole that is identical in both pieces of wood.

The wood of the top rung had been planed smooth by hand along both edges. It also had four strange holes that were not needed in making the ladder. Koehler decided the plank had once been used as flooring, probably in an attic or garage.

SETTING UP EVIDENCE

Part of the ransom money was paid in special gold certificates. The police thought this might help them trace the notes, if they were spent, and find the kidnapper. The ploy worked. A suspicious garage worker wrote down the license plate number of a man who passed him one of the special $10 bills. He gave it to the police. They traced the owner of the car to a Bruno Richard Hauptmann, a German man with a criminal record. He lived in the Bronx.

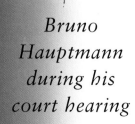

Bruno Hauptmann during his court hearing

THE RANSOM NOTE

The ransom note also provided clues. It was poorly written, with many mistakes. Handwriting experts said it had been written by someone foreign who didn't speak English very well—probably someone from Germany—and was poorly educated.

STATE OF NEW YORK—DEPARTMENT OF TAXATION AND FINANCE—BUREAU OF MOTOR VEHICLES
APPLICATION FOR REGISTRATION
1934 PASSENGER VEHICLE
NOT USED FOR HIRE
Use Special Blank on and after July 1st
1. Print Name of owner RICHARD HAUPTMAN IV
APP. FEB
REG. NO.

RICHARD   HAUPTMAN IV
RICHARD   HAUPTMANN

Clues in the handwriting: at the top is Hauptmann's signature on a car registration form. Below that is the same signature made up from letters cut out of the ransom note. The ransom note is on the left.

MR. CHAS. LINBERG,
YOUR BABY IS SAFE BUT HE IS NOT USING NO MEDICINES. HE IS EATING PORK CHOP. PORK AND BEANS JUST WHAT WE EAT. JUST FOLOW OUR DIRECTION AND HAVE ONE HUNDRED THOUSEND BUCKS READY IN VERY SHORT TIME THATS JUST WHAT WE NEED
YOURS B. H.

CONVICTED

Handwriting experts found a good match between Hauptmann's handwriting and the ransom note. It was more evidence against him.

Hauptmann was convicted on the evidence of the ladder, the note, and the money. Although he continued to claim innocence, Hauptmann was sent to the electric chair in 1936.

BOBBY GREENLEASE

On September 28, 1953, Bonnie Heady arrived at Bobby Greenlease's school in Kansas City, Missouri. She said the six-year-old's mother was in the hospital, and she had come to pick him up. But it wasn't true.

Heady and her boyfriend, Carl Hall, drove the boy into the countryside and shot him. They buried the body in Heady's garden and sent a ransom note to Bobby's father demanding $600,000. They fled with the money, without saying where Bobby was.

CAUGHT!

Heady and Hall got drunk and let other people know they had money. Hall was soon arrested and admitted to the kidnapping, but not to killing Bobby.

EVIDENCE

The forensic evidence was the bloodstains and Hall's gun. Bloodstains found in Heady's house on a blouse and a rug matched Bobby's blood.

School friends of Bobby Greenlease pray for him.

16

A forensic scientist uses a microscope to compare two bullet casings. One is from a crime scene, the other is from the gun of a suspect. If the markings match, this would be important evidence linking the suspect to the crime.

The FBI laboratory showed that shell casings found in the house had been fired from Hall's .38 caliber snub-nosed Smith & Wesson revolver. A lead bullet on the floor mat of Heady's car had been fired from the same gun. The evidence convicted both Heady and Hall. They were executed for the crime.

CLUES FROM GUNS

The forensic study of firearms is known as ballistics. Each gun barrel is different. It has a spiral groove etched into it that gives a bullet its spin. This improves the gun's accuracy. As the bullet comes out of the barrel, the groove leaves marks on the bullet called **striations**. Ballistics experts use these to show whether a bullet was fired from a particular gun. The shell casing is ejected when the bullet is fired. This, too, is marked by parts inside the gun and can be matched to a particular gun.

GRAEME THORNE

Graeme Thorne was eight years old when his parents won the lottery in New South Wales, Australia. It was not as lucky as it seemed. The boy was kidnapped on his way to school in Sydney on July 7, 1960. The kidnappers made a ransom demand by phone. This was Australia's first kidnapping for ransom.

Some of Graeme's belongings turned up during the following week, but there was nothing from the kidnappers. His body was found wrapped in a rug five weeks later.

Graeme Thorne (top) and his father Basil Thorne

HAIRS, DIRT, AND PLANTS

Graeme's clothes were crusted with a pink substance like soil. His clothing and the rug were covered in hairs, and mold was growing on his socks and shoes. Bits of sticks and leaves were found on his clothing. This **trace evidence** was all the police had to go on.

Investigators also noticed that one tassel was missing from the fringe on the rug. The tassel would turn out to be important.

CALLING ALL EXPERTS

The forensics team called on experts from different fields to help them. A fungus expert found four different types of mold on Graeme's shoes and socks. The molds were about six weeks old. That meant Graeme had been killed soon after he was kidnapped.

A medical officer found four types of hair on the rug and clothing from three people and a dog. He said it was almost certainly a Pekingese dog.

The curator of the Geological and Mining Museum in The Rocks, New South Wales, identified the pink dust as a type of **mortar** often used in house construction in Australia. There was also a lot of plant material—sticks, leaves, and seeds.

SCANNING ELECTRON MICROSCOPES

To the naked eye, the samples of mortar, plant material, and hairs would be impossible to tell apart from similar samples. However, forensic scientists found clear distinguishing features in the samples by using a scanning **electron** microscope. This works by firing a beam of electrons at the sample and measuring its shape and edges. This information is converted into a picture. For forensic work, the microscope usually magnifies items by 10,000 times.

A laboratory technician uses a scanning electron microscope.

The plant samples taken from the rug and clothing included a seed of this rare type of cypress tree, known as the sawara cypress.

Each bit of plant material was carefully removed. The scientific staff of the National Herbarium set to work on the case. They identified each plant sample. One was a very rare cypress seed. It was a type of tree that did not grow anywhere near where Graeme's body was found. This was a vital clue.

PUBLIC APPEAL
Police turned to the public for help. Did anyone know of a housing development with pink mortar and rare cypress trees? A postman suggested a house on his route. It had the right type of mortar and the rare trees. The garden also had many of the other plants identified from the trace evidence.

A MAN AND HIS DOG

The people who lived in the house had only just moved in. The last tenant, Stephen Bradley, had moved out on the day of the kidnapping. Neighbors said he had a Pekingese dog. He had driven a car similar to one seen outside the Thornes' house on the morning of the kidnapping. A photo left in the house showed Bradley having a picnic on the rug that Graeme had been wrapped in. Police even found the missing tassel on the floor.

HAIR OF THE DOG

Animal hairs are covered in tiny scales, which make up patterns along the length of the hair. The thickness and color of the hairs and the shape of the hair help experts identify animal hairs. DNA testing can also match hairs to a particular animal, just as DNA analysis can match samples from a person.

Bradley had sold his car, left his dog, and taken a ship to England. Police found the car and dog. Pink dust in the car and hair samples from the dog matched the trace evidence. Bradley was flown back to Australia. He was sentenced to life in prison.

Stephen Bradley

21

MARILYN MILLER

Marilyn Miller was a 15-year-old girl from Kings County, California. She was taken from her bedroom on March 21, 1962. There was no ransom note or any indication of why she had been taken. Her body was found a few hours later in a reservoir near her home. Police found tire tracks and footprints on a dirt road nearby. They also found a pair of workman's gloves. One of Marilyn's friends remembered seeing a black and turquoise car parked near her house. There were no other clues.

FIND THE CAR, FIND THE CULPRIT

Police soon found the abandoned car nearby. They also found the boots that had made the footprints. One of the boots had been repaired using the heel from a different boot. This was lucky—it meant it made unique prints, so the police could be certain they had the right boots.

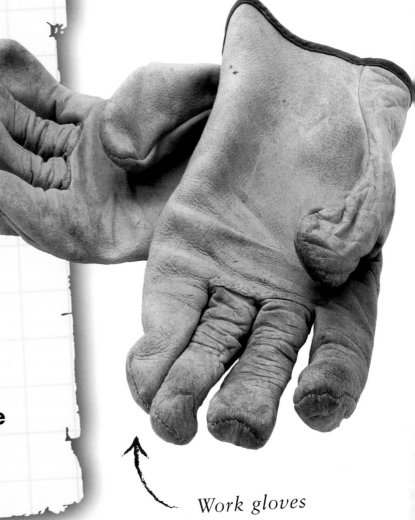

Work gloves

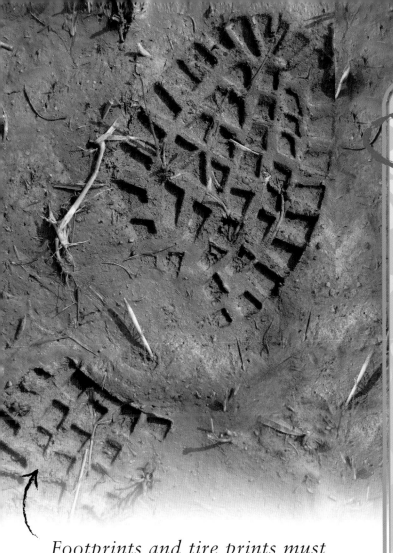

CAST IN STONE

Forensic detectives photograph tire prints and footprints and take impressions of them. These are often made using the plaster that dentists use to cast **impressions** of teeth. It is a fine grade plaster that reveals all details of the print. If the wet plaster is poured in carefully, the print can be lifted completely. Prints can even be obtained from dust or sand.

A newer method uses gel lifters. A gel lifter can be used to pick up footprints not visible to the naked eye. Gel can even lift a print from a clean shoe on a sheet of paper. A sheet of special gel is laid over the print, left for a few minutes, and then peeled away. By shining a light on it from the side, forensics experts can view details of the print left on the gel.

Footprints and tire prints must be recorded quickly if they are to be used as evidence or else they will be lost.

The car was registered to a local man, Brooker Hillery. He had just been released from jail for another crime. Police showed that the gloves they had found also belonged to Hillery. He was soon tried, convicted, and sentenced to death.

AVOIDING HIS FATE

Hillery dragged out the process as long as possible, launching one appeal after another, until the death sentence was ruled unconstitutional in 1972. Although the death sentence was brought back in 1975, Hillery's sentence had already been changed to imprisonment. In 1978, Hillery asked for a **retrial**, hoping to be released.

OLD EVIDENCE, NEW METHODS

Most of the original witnesses had died in the 16 years since Hillery's first trial. The prosecution looked for new evidence. They found it in Marilyn's bedroom and Hillery's car.

Police had kept dust vacuumed from Marilyn's bedroom floor.

CLUES IN THE PAINT

Forensic scientists examined the particles of paint found on Marilyn's bedroom floor. The particles were round in shape. The scientists knew that when paint is sprayed onto a surface, the drops flatten. These drops were tiny balls. They had not fallen onto a hard surface. They also had fibers stuck to them. The paint had fallen onto fabric—Hillery's clothes.

They now examined it under a microscope and found tiny particles of blue paint.

Hillery had refused to let police sell his car, so it was still in the car pound. Investigators found paint inside it that matched the drops from Marilyn's room. The police still had Hillery's clothes from the night of the abduction. They found matching paint on his clothes.

Hillery had sprayed the inside of his car, and some paint had fallen onto his clothes. In his struggle with Marilyn, tiny particles of dried paint had fallen onto the floor of the car. After 25 years, Hillery was convicted of the crime again, but techniques were used that had not been developed when he committed the crime.

A forensic scientist compares paint chips from a car involved in a crime with known samples of paint. Finding a match helps to identify the car.

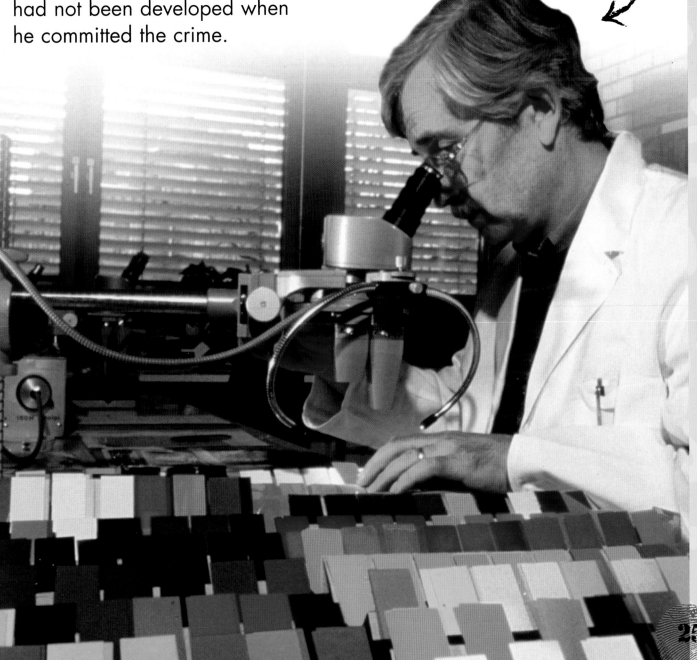

PATTY HEARST

Patty Hearst, the daughter of a multimillionaire businessman, was kidnapped from her home in California by two armed men and a woman on February 4, 1974. She was 19 years old. They carried her, kicking and screaming, to their car.

Patty Hearst is caught on surveillance camera during a bank robbery in San Francisco.

The kidnappers were members of a small group called the Symbionese Liberation Army (SLA). They demanded the release of two of their members from prison in return for Hearst. The demand was refused. They asked instead that her family give millions of dollars to feed the poor in California. The family paid some money, but the kidnappers said it was not enough. Hearst was next seen holding up a bank in April 1974. It seemed she had joined her kidnappers' cause.

ARREST THE VICTIM!

The bank robbery netted $10,000. Hearst was clearly visible on security films. In a strange turnaround, the kidnap victim was now wanted by police. The FBI next found Hearst shooting randomly outside a sporting goods store where she was trying to free a member of the SLA caught shoplifting.

In Hearst's abandoned getaway car, the police found a parking ticket that led them to the SLA's hideout. In a dramatic shoot-out and fire, six members of the SLA died. Hearst went on the run, but was caught in September 1975.

GOOD GIRL GONE BAD?

At Patty Hearst's trial, the jurors had to decide whether she had willingly joined the SLA or been brainwashed, as she claimed. For this, help was needed from **forensic psychologists**.

On May 17, 1974, Los Angeles police surrounded the SLA's safe house and ordered them to surrender. During the ensuing gun battle, the house erupted in flames, and six SLA members died.

FORENSIC PSYCHOLOGY

Forensic psychologists know about normal patterns of behavior and the behavior of people with mental illnesses. They know how people act under stress and in other difficult situations. They use their knowledge of how people act and think to assess the person they are examining. Often, they must decide whether a person knew what they were doing. Criminals sometimes plead insanity. This means they were not sane at the time and should not be held responsible for what they did.

Was Patty Hearst responsible or had she been brainwashed? The details of her kidnapping and how she was held became the subject of the investigation. Hearst said that her kidnappers kept her gagged and blindfolded in a dark closet for 57 days. They abused her, shouted at her, kept her from sleeping, and gave her very little food. They wore her down so that she would do as they told her.

TAPED MESSAGES

Working with Hearst and taped messages sent to the media and footage from the bank's security camera, forensic psychologists had to decide whether she was telling the truth. Hearst said she was given a choice—join the SLA or die. But in a tape released by the kidnappers, Hearst says she was offered a different choice—join them or be released in a safe area. According to the tape, she had chosen to join them and fight for the "freedom of all oppressed people." She took a new name, Tania, and became an SLA terrorist. Whether or not it was by choice was for investigators to find out.

Patty Hearst on her way to court during her trial on a charge of bank robbery

STOCKHOLM SYNDROME

Hearst's lawyers claimed that she had been brainwashed and had developed Stockholm Syndrome. In this condition, kidnap victims become sympathetic to their kidnappers. They come to support their captors' cause and may defend them.

Hearst was found guilty of bank robbery. She was imprisoned for her crimes as part of the SLA but was released two years later.

PSYCHOLOGICAL TESTING

Forensic psychologists begin by running a set of tests on the person they are investigating. These reveal the person's level of intelligence, how well their brain controls their body, and their personality type. Other tests are designed to show whether a person is lying. If a person claims to be suffering from a particular condition, tests can show whether his or her symptoms and behavior match the condition.

A lawyer for the prosecution holds up a photo of Patty Hearst holding a gun.

29

ALDO MORO

Aldo Moro was a leading Italian politician who had been prime minister twice. On March 16, 1978, he was driving through Rome when armed attackers caused his car to crash. His five bodyguards were killed, and he was dragged away. An extreme political group called the Red Brigades claimed responsibility and said they were holding Moro. They demanded the release of terrorist prisoners in exchange for the politician, but the Italian government refused. Moro wrote several letters asking the government to negotiate, but this had no effect.

Moro was held for 54 days. Then his kidnappers put him in the car, shot him, and put his body into the trunk. They abandoned the car in Rome.

Aldo Moro in a photo taken after his kidnapping. The flag of the Red Brigades is in the background.

BULLET CASES

At the scene of the kidnapping, police found bullet casings. Forensic experts could tell they came from a rare type of gun made in the Soviet Union. This was solid evidence of the involvement of the Red Brigades, who were supplied with weapons by the Soviet Union.

A forensic geologist grinds up a soil sample for analysis. Particular types of rock and microscopic plants and animals can help to link a suspect to a crime scene.

WHERE WAS HE HELD?

When Moro's body was discovered, police found grains of sand and microscopic fossils in his clothes. They traced these to a stretch of beach north of Rome. They also found traces of resins used in boat building. These supported the theory that he had been held near a beach.

Despite all the evidence, experts have never been able to determine what happened to Moro. Several members of the Red Brigades spent time in jail for the kidnapping and murder, but the precise sequence of events remains a mystery.

FORENSIC GEOLOGY

Forensic geologists look very closely at samples of soil, rock, or sand to determine where they came from. Sand is made of rock, broken into very tiny pieces. It can contain tiny fossils, too. Sand samples from different beaches have distinctive fragments of different sizes and rocks of different types. Forensic geologists use microscopes to investigate the composition of soil, sand, and rock to match samples that show a victim or suspect has been in a particular place.

DON TIDEY

On November 24, 1983, supermarket executive Don Tidey was taking his daughter to school in the Ardoyne area of North Belfast, Ireland. On the way, he stopped at what seemed to be a police checkpoint. These were common in Northern Ireland at the time. But the people who stopped Tidey were not the police. They were members of an extreme group known as the Irish Republican Army (IRA). They forced Tidey into a car at gunpoint.

Brendan McFarlane

CSIs gathered evidence to prove that the escaped kidnappers had been in the hideout. They collected items, photographed the objects, and recorded the fingerprints.

SHOOT-OUT

A few days later, the kidnappers sent Tidey's photo and a ransom demand to his employers. Police rescued Tidey in a shoot-out after 23 days in captivity. Two security officers were killed in the rescue, but all the kidnappers escaped.

EVIDENCE LOST

It would be a long time before the police could use their evidence. One of the kidnappers, Brendan McFarlane, was charged in 1998. This was 15 years after the crime was committed. By this time, the police had lost the objects with the fingerprints, so McFarlane objected to the trial. In 2006, the court ruled that the fingerprint records and photographs could be used at trial.

MODERN FINGERPRINTING

CSIs now have more methods for lifting fingerprints than dusting them with powder. These include lights that show up invisible marks, chemicals to reveal fingerprints, and a device called a Kelvin probe. This measures variations in **electrical** **conductivity** over a surface and makes an image from the readings. It is a good way of capturing fingerprints from metal surfaces.

Fingerprints are now stored in a computer database. Police can search millions of fingerprints in a few seconds to find a match. This task would have taken far longer using paper records of fingerprints.

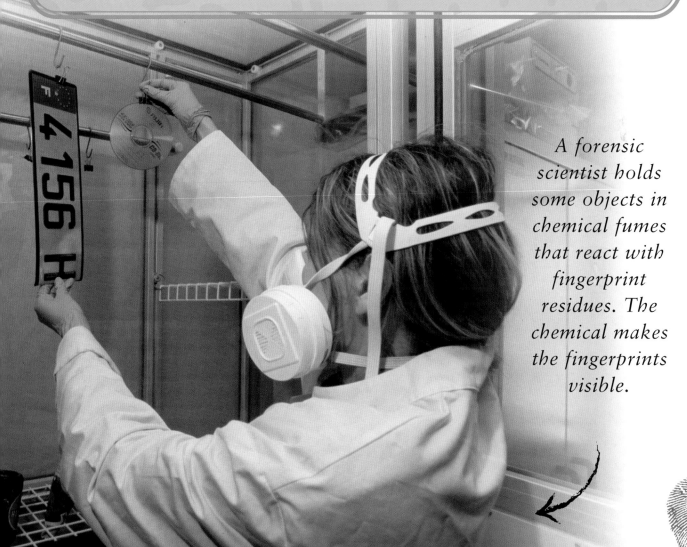

A forensic scientist holds some objects in chemical fumes that react with fingerprint residues. The chemical makes the fingerprints visible.

SHARI SMITH

Shari Smith

On May 31, 1985, Shari Smith, aged 18, from Lexington County, South Carolina, stopped her car in her driveway to put a letter in her mail box. Minutes later, her father found the car with the door open and the engine running, but Shari was gone.

Later the same day, her kidnapper phoned her house. He used an electronic device to distort his voice so that it could not be recognized. The next day, he sent a letter written by Smith. He made more calls, but finally told the family where her body could be found. On the day of her funeral, he made a final call to describe in detail how he had killed her.

LITTLE EVIDENCE

Smith had been dead long enough for some forensic evidence to have been lost. The letter had been written by the victim. And although police had a recording, the kidnapper had disguised his voice. They turned to forensic psychologists to build a profile of the man they were looking for.

BUILDING A PICTURE

The FBI Signal Analysis Unit worked out that the kidnapper had used a variable speed control device to distort his voice. This suggested that he had a background in electronics. Psychologists examined the wording of the messages, the few known details of the crime, and the fact that the kidnapper enjoyed tormenting the family. Working from these details and knowledge about people who had committed similar crimes in the past, forensic psychologists built a profile of the kidnapper.

GETTING INSIDE THE CRIMINAL MIND

Forensic psychologists build a psychological profile from all the information they can gather about the criminal from the crime. From knowledge of previous crimes and criminals, they determine the type of person that probably carried out the act. The profile can be quite detailed, giving the age, level of education, preferences, lifestyle, and some aspects of the criminal's physical appearance.

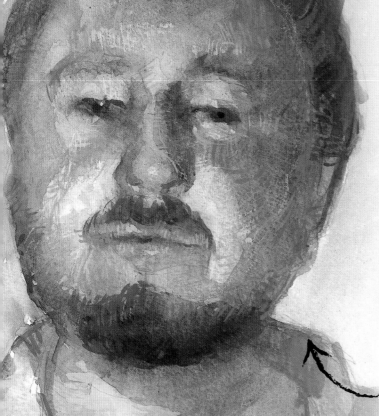

They said the man was in his twenties or thirties. He was overweight, not attractive, probably separated after an unsuccessful marriage, and had a history of making obscene phone calls. When they caught Larry Gene Bell, these details turned out to be accurate.

Larry Gene Bell

35

SHEDDING LIGHT ON THE CASE

Investigators looking at the note written by Smith made a breakthrough. They used a device that finds impressions on paper. Using microscopic analysis, this machine shows up tiny dents in the paper that cannot be

This device, called an oscilloscope, converts the speaker's voice to a pattern. It can be used to compare a voice and a recording.

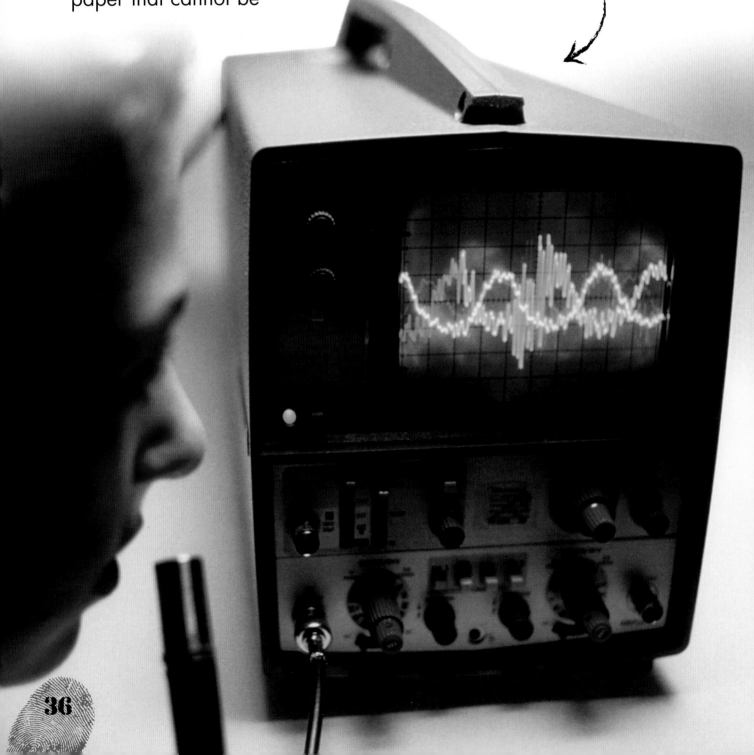

seen with the naked eye. The investigators found that another sheet of paper in the pad, resting on this one, had been used to write a grocery list and a phone number.

The phone number belonged to a middle-aged couple. They had been on vacation when the crime was committed, but they had allowed their handyman to live in the house while they were away. The handyman matched the profile the psychologists had made. Detectives had a recording of the final call the kidnapper had made to the Smith family in which he had not disguised his voice. They played it to the couple, who recognized the voice of their handyman, Larry Gene Bell.

LICKED

A final piece of evidence proved Bell's connection with the case. Forensics experts recovered a sample of his DNA from the stamp he had licked to put on the letter to Smith's parents. It matched a sample police took

from Bell on his arrest. Bell was tried and found guilty of Smith's kidnapping and murder. He was executed in 1996.

VOICE ANALYSIS

Forensic scientists use a voice **spectrograph** to identify voices. The machine records a trace—a line that goes up and down with the **frequency of sounds** in a recording. Many parts of the body contribute to a person's voice, including all of the mouth, the throat, and parts of the chest. Each voice produces different, distinctive patterns. Experts use voiceprints in the same way as fingerprints to prove someone's identity. If necessary, sophisticated sound-enhancing techniques are used to make a voice louder or to remove background noise or distortion.

BEN NEEDHAM

Ben Needham was playing at his grandmother's house in Kos, Greece, on July 24, 1991, when he vanished. Police treated the family as the main suspects and did not follow up their only lead—an older boy seen in a shop with Ben in the evening. No ransom was demanded and Ben was never found. His family believes he was stolen for illegal adoption or sale.

Ben Needham at 21 months, shortly before he was abducted.

FALSE HOPES

In 1998, a man on vacation saw a blond boy of about 10 playing on the beach of another Greek island, Rhodes. He was suspicious, as few Greek children are blond. He took a photo and ruffled the boy's hair to get a sample, which he took to police. DNA tests on the hair and on samples from Ben they had on file proved the boy was not Ben.

FACE OF THE FUTURE

It is now many years since Ben disappeared. If he is still alive, he will look very different. To help the search for Ben, police scientists have produced "aged" images of him. The first of these was released when Ben would have been 13 years old. Five years later, they produced a picture of Ben as experts believe he would look at 18.

A computer-generated image of Ben Needham as experts think he might look at 18.

AGE PROGRESSION

Aged images of children are created using photos taken at the time the child disappeared and photos of his or her parents as children. The image is based on the parent the child most looks like. A complex computer program "ages" the child using elements from the parents' photos and known facts about how the face changes during aging. Details such as hairstyle, glasses, and clothes are added later and selected from a gallery.

Forensic aging programs can take many factors into account. These include diet, alcohol and smoking habits, exercise, job type, and psychological makeup.

JONBENÉT RAMSEY

JonBenét Ramsey was a six-year-old girl from Boulder, Colorado. Her mother found a ransom note on the stairs of their home before she knew her daughter was missing. It seemed that JonBenét had been snatched on December 26, 1996, from her bedroom. The ransom demand was for $118,000—the amount her wealthy father had received as a bonus.

Police searched the house and found nothing. A few hours later, her father found JonBenét's body in the wine cellar. She had been killed by blows to the head and strangled with a **garrote** made from a cord and the handle of a paintbrush.

JonBenét Ramsey

RUINED EVIDENCE

The police in Boulder had little experience with kidnappings. They did not secure the crime scene quickly as they should have done. Many people —police, family, and friends—moved around the house for hours. This destroyed large amounts of trace evidence such as footprints and fingerprints. JonBenét's father had found and moved her body and removed duct tape from her mouth before police had a chance to photograph the body in its original position. There was very little useful evidence left to work with.

STRANGE RANSOM

The strange amount demanded as ransom was not the only odd thing about the note. Other details seemed to suggest the person who wrote it knew the family, including a reference to a naval base JonBenét's father had been at.

This is part of the ransom note sent to JonBenét's parents.

money and hence a earlier delivery pick-up of your daughter. Any deviation of my instructions will result in the immediate execution of your daughter. You will also be denied her remains for proper burial. The two gentlemen watching over your daughter do not particularly like you so I advise you not to provoke them. Speaking to anyone about your situation, such as Police, F.B.I., etc., will result in your daughter being beheaded. If we catch you talking to a stray dog, she dies. If you alert bank authorities, she dies. If the money is in any way marked or tampered with, she dies. You will be scanned for electronic devices and if any are found, she dies. You can try to

HANDWRITING ANALYSIS

Everyone has their own style of handwriting. Forensic handwriting experts look at the shape of the letters, the force with which the writer presses on the paper, the thickness of the strokes, any distinctive features, and other aspects of handwriting. They use their findings to compare documents and decide whether they were written by the same person. They can often do this even if the criminal has tried to disguise his or her writing.

The note was written on paper taken from their home. The investigators also found a partially written practice note. Experts said this showed the kidnapper was not a sophisticated criminal. Ransom notes are usually prepared in advance. They are also usually typed to avoid later handwriting analysis.

41

PARENTS AS SUSPECTS

For some time, police suspected JonBenét's parents—particularly her mother—had killed JonBenét. Some experts thought her handwriting matched the ransom note. Fibers from her jacket were found under the duct tape over JonBenét's mouth. But the head of the FBI's Behavioral Science Unit decided this was not likely. He said the crime was probably carried out by an intruder.

John and Patsy Ramsey at a press conference in 2000

Forensic psychologists said details about the body did suggest the parents killed her. The body was indoors. They said a parent would not want to put their child's body outside, but an intruder would not want to leave evidence in the house. The body was partly covered, which suggested some sympathy with the victim and perhaps **remorse**. The way JonBenét had been killed—from behind—might have been a way to avoid looking at her while killing her. In 2008, DNA

John Mark Karr falsely confessed to being with JonBenét when she died.

her death had been an accident. Handwriting experts said his writing was similar to that of the ransom note. In particular, he shared a rare way of forming the letters E, M, and T. DNA tests did not match him to traces found on JonBenét's body, and he was not charged.

evidence finally cleared JonBenét's parents completely. The police believe a person still unknown killed her.

FALSE TRAIL

In 2006, police found John Mark Karr in Thailand. He had sent e-mails that he had been with JonBenét when she died but that

DNA PROFILING

DNA profiling can be used to prove that biological evidence is from a particular person. DNA is found in all body cells. It is present in saliva, blood, and other body fluids. From the tiniest drop of blood or a single hair, forensic scientists can take enough DNA to identify a person if they have a sample from the suspect. In the future, scientists will be able to come up with a physical description of someone from their DNA that includes hair color, eye color, skin color, and likely height.

TIME LINE

ca. **1590**	The microscope is invented in the Netherlands.
1752	The first case of an expert witness giving evidence in a European court. Dr. Anthony Addington uses a chemical test to prove that an accused poisoner had the arsenic in his home.
1828	Kaspar Hauser appears—apparently after being kidnapped for most of his life.
1874	Four-year-old Charlie Brewster Ross is kidnapped. This is the first known U.S. kidnapping for ransom. The kidnappers are later killed carrying out an unrelated crime. The boy is never found.
1894	Fingerprinting is first used as a means of identification in Britain.
1901	Sir Edward R. Henry develops a system of fingerprint classification that is accepted by Scotland Yard, the headquarters of the British police.
1901	Karl Landsteiner of Austria discovers the different blood groups.
1910	Edmond Locard sets up the first police crime laboratory in France.
1915	Italian Leone Lattes discovers how to identify the blood group of dried blood.
1929	New techniques for identifying guns and bullets, developed by Calvin Goddard, are used to solve the St. Valentine's Day Massacre in Chicago, Illinois.
1932	Charles Lindbergh Jr. is kidnapped and killed.
1933	The electron microscope is invented.

1953 James Watson and Francis Crick describe the structure of DNA.

1960 Eight-year-old Graeme Thorne is kidnapped in Australia's first kidnapping for ransom.

1973 John Paul Getty III, 16-year-old son of a billionaire, is kidnapped in Italy. The kidnappers demand $17 million. When they do not get it, they cut off Getty's ear and send it to the family, threatening to return the boy in bits. The ransom is paid. The kidnappers have never been caught.

1973 Bank workers in Stockholm, Sweden, are kidnapped for five days. The victims become attached to their kidnappers. This is the first known example of Stockholm Syndrome.

1974 Patty Hearst is kidnapped. She then joins her kidnappers' terrorist organization, the Symbionese Liberation Army.

1975 Eleven OPEC ministers are kidnapped in Austria. OPEC is an organization of oil-producing countries.

1980s Computerized databases of fingerprints make it much easier to search stored fingerprints to match a newly collected fingerprint.

1984 DNA profiling is developed as a way of matching suspects or victims to DNA from trace evidence.

1988 DNA profiling is first used to convict the British murderer and rapist Colin Pitchfork.

1995–6 Marc Dutroux kidnaps and murders several girls in Belgium. The poor handling of the case leads to a complete reorganization of the Belgian police service.

2006 Natascha Kampusch escapes. She had been kidnapped and held prisoner for eight years by Wolfgang Priklopil in Austria.

GLOSSARY

crime scene
The place where a crime has been carried out.

crime scene investigator (CSI)
Person who collects evidence at the scene of a crime.

dispute
Serious disagreement or argument.

DNA
The genetic material that carries the information defining all the characteristics of an individual. DNA is present in almost all body cells. Each person (except identical twins) has unique DNA, so it can be used to match a sample to a suspect or victim.

dungeon
An unpleasant prison, often underground and without windows.

electrical conductivity
The ability of a material to carry electricity.

electron
Part of an atom, the smallest particle of matter

evidence
Things or facts that prove something

expert witness
A person with advanced skills in a particular field who presents evidence in a criminal case.

fingerprint
Mark that shows the pattern of ridges on the fingertip.

forensic psychologist
Medical expert who helps to investigate crimes and criminals using the knowledge of human behavior and how the mind works.

frequency of sound
The rate of vibration in a sound. Sounds travel as waves through the air, like ripples over the surface of water. The frequency measures the interval between the tops of the waves.

garrote
A rope or cord that is put around the victim's neck and tightened by twisting with a rod or stick to strangle the victim.

hanged
Killed by breaking the neck or strangling by tying a rope around the neck and suddenly dropping (or raising) the victim.

hostage
Someone who has been taken against their will and is held prisoner until an agreement is made, often to pay money or release other prisoners.

impression
mark left in or on a surface

latent fingerprint
A fingerprint left as invisible traces of oil and dirt on a surface.

lift
Take an impression of a fingerprint from a surface.

milling machine
A machine with a rotating cutter used for cutting wood to shape.

mortar
Substance used to adhere bricks together. It is a powder that is mixed with water.

negotiate
To talk about a problem to try and reach an agreement.

ransom
Money (or something else) that is demanded in exchange for releasing someone who has been kidnapped.

remorse
Feeling of sorrow and regret at having done something bad.

retrial
Another trial that replaces the earlier legal trial.

sample
A small amount of a substance.

saw mill
A place where trees are cut up ready to be sold as lumber.

spectrograph
A graph drawn as a wiggly line showing the variation of something (such as sound) over time.

striations
Marks left on a bullet by the parallel grooves inside a gun barrel.

terrorist
Person who tries to achieve a political aim by carrying out violent acts intended to frighten their enemies.

trace evidence
Tiny amounts of a substance left at a crime scene

victim
A person who has suffered some bad experience.

FURTHER INFORMATION

BOOKS
Forensic Science by Chris Cooper (DK Publishing, 2008)
Forensic Science by Alex Frith (Usborne, 2007)
Careers in Criminal Profiling by Janey Levy (Rosen Central, 2008)
The DNA Gave It Away! by Yvonne Morrison (Children's Press, 2007)
Forensics by Richard Platt (Kingfisher Books, 2005)

WEB SITES
http://www.charleslindbergh.com/kidnap/index.asp
This site provides biographical information about Charles Lindbergh and the kidnapping of his son.

www.fbi.gov/kids/
The stages of an FBI investigation of a crime shown step-by-step with links to further information on the forensic techniques used.

science.howstuffworks.com/csi5.htm
Crime scene investigation techniques explained in detail. You can also tour a crime lab virtually.

www.trutv.com/library/crime/
A full database of major crimes and how they were solved, including some of the kidnapping cases covered in this book.

http://www.virtualmuseum.ca/
This site explains terms used in forensics, a time line, and a crime to solve virtually.

INDEX